Dear Granddaughter
Life Lessons from Your Grandmother

Written by Judy Smith

Photography by Lou Guarracino

Dear Granddaughter,

There are many life lessons you won't appreciate until you are near my age. I had so many dreams of the person I wanted to be and through it all, I never took the time to be the woman I already was. One day, shortly after I turned 50, I realized that I was indeed the woman I had aspired to be. I no longer felt the need to be more, have more, and want more. I came to the understanding that I truly liked who I was and I no longer felt the urge to continue the search for a "new me."

On your journey to self-discovery, you will go through many phases and levels. The wonderful poem, "When I am an Old Woman", tells a beautiful story of accepting yourself and not caring how other's view you. Over time the poem will have deeper meaning to you. When it does, you will understand why your grandmother often wears "A purple hat with a red dress".

I love you dearly.

When I am an Old Woman

I shall wear purple

With a red hat which doesn't go, and doesn't suit me.

And I shall spend my pension on brandy and summer gloves

And satin sandals, and say we've no money for butter

I shall sit down on the pavement when I'm tired

And gobble up samples in shops and press alarm bells

And run my stick along the public railings

And make up for the sobriety of my youth.

I shall go out in my slippers in the rain

And pick the flowers in other people's gardens

And learn to spit.

You can wear terrible shirts and grow more fat

And eat three pounds of sausages at a go

Or only bread and pickles for a week.

And hoard pens and pencils and beermats and things in boxes.

But now we must have clothes that keep us dry

And pay our rent and not swear in the street

And set a good example for my children.

We will have friends to dinner and read the papers.

But maybe I ought to practice a little now?

So people who know me are not too shocked and surprised

When suddenly I am old and start to wear purple.

Jenny Joseph

Rejoice in Your Individuality

No one else is exactly like you.

Live Simply

Practice the art of
feng shui by arranging
things around your
home and office
that will relax and
energize you.

Have Order in Your Life

Order will invite calmness which precedes clear thought.
When we have clear thoughts, we can make room in
our lives for happiness and success.

Declutter

A sense of calm and joy lightens your heart when clutter
is removed from your environment.

Nourish Your Soul

Coming together with your family at the table is more than just enjoying the meal. This is where the bounty of the meal makes the body strong while the comfort of family and friends around us fills us with warmth and fortifies the soul.

- *Always have fresh garlic on hand.*

- *Grow fresh herbs on your window sill.*

- *Use good china for everyday use.*

- *Make a tradition of Sunday dinners with your family and extended family as often as possible.*

- *Add a pinch of cinnamon to your coffee.*

- *Add food with wonderful colors to your diet.*

Sow the Seeds of Your Desire

Quiet reflection can be found while enjoying the benefits of gardening. This teaches you to be patient for the bounty of the next crop and in the next cycle of your life.

Seek Essential Wealth

Follow your inner heart and pursue a career that brings you passion and happiness and you will indeed reap the rewards of success. When we follow our authentic path, we are using the gifts that have been bestowed upon us. By seeking wonder and exploring your passions, the money will follow.

Live the Lifestyle

Mentally live the lifestyle you desire. Subscribe to financial magazines, indulge in scanning glamorous catalogs. Always remember:

- *What you save is more important than what you earn.*
- *Share your good fortune with others who need it.*
- *Respect the things you have and avoid waste.*

Come Play with Me

Even as adults we need "recess" and down time to escape our everyday chores and responsibilities. Children play with complete abandon and nothing else is on their minds. It is important as an adult to return to this behavior from time to time.

Tea My Dear?

Plan a tea party with a friend once a month. Indulge in delectable croissants, pastries and specialty teas. Use your favorite linen napkins, teapot and tea cups. It's also fun to dress for the occasion with party gloves and hats.

Mirror, Mirror. . .
Discover Your Own Beauty

A beautiful woman is one who values herself physically, mentally, emotionally and spiritually. To be a complete person, develop your inner beauty. As we age and create a stronger sense of self, our spiritual self becomes more beautiful radiating confidence with grace and reassurance.

Age Exquisitely

- Be kind to your body.

- Protect yourself from the sun.

- Stay fit…take up yoga.

- Follow the lead of women you admire and let them be your guide.

Enjoy Fine Things

Spray your sheets with perfume, use linen napkins and find
embroidered treasures at flea markets.

Embrace Yourself

Flaws and all!
Allow your imperfections to be part of your beauty.

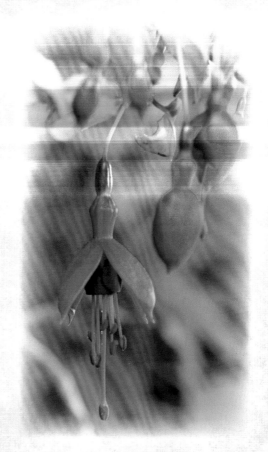

Spiritual Retreat

Treat yourself to a massage
often. It not only reduces
stress, it makes you glow with
a feeling of well being.

Indulge in Bubbles

Water cleanses, soothes and restores. Aromatherapy candles are the ideal complement to luxury and calmness. Add your favorite essential oils to your bath. The oils will seep into your respiratory and skin to reduce stress and evoke a good night's sleep.

Finding Grace

When things are
not going as you
had planned or
hoped, learn to
go with the flow.
Events that at
first seem
to be unfortunate
or undesirable
may actually
provide you with
surprising results
and advantages.

Love Sweet Love

Love is as natural and vital to life as breathing. It is as crucial for your mind and body as the air you breathe. The more connected you are to the people you love in your life, the healthier you will be physically and emotionally.

- *Love is complete peace and excruciating, almost unbearable joy and the deep passionate sense of being "home".*

- *True love is unconditional where we accept each other's flaws and embrace each other's differences.*

- *Love conquers all…however, you must surrender to it first.*

Learning to love fully is the greatest accomplishment we can make in our lives. Love all things and all people in your life lavishly. Love your family, your friends, your work and yourself.

Forgiveness – C'est la Vie

It is inevitable that you will be hurt, scorned and disappointed by the actions of others. While you cannot control the deeds of others, you have total control over what you allow the actions of others to do to you. Learn to move past the negative vibrations by projecting loving kindness to the person who is hurting you. This will counteract the hurt and negativity resulting in beneficial healing.

By seeing how a painful situation has helped you grow, you will reconnect with your inner self with peace and serenity.

Forgive Yourself First

Mistakes hurt our self-esteem when we aim to be perfect.
No one gets through life without making a few mistakes.

Count Your Blessings

- Every day reflect on three things for which you are grateful.

- Keep a journal and allow your deepest thoughts to be expressed.

- Say thank you to the people in your life – often!

- Be mindful of your blessings. Strive to be aware of all aspects of your personal, professional and family life for which you are grateful.

Art of Gratitude

Happiness, sadness, heartbreak and excitement all come in and out of our lives. The true secret is learning to give thanks for each of them. For it is through the emotions we feel, that we are able to appreciate and honor the positive things that we encounter. If we did not know pain, would we know joy? If we never experienced emptiness, would we ever truly know fulfillment?

Acceptance

When you accept a difficult situation this does not mean you agree
with it, only that you understand you are not able to change it.
You can only change how you allow it to affect you.

Detach Yourself from Criticism

Respond in a calm and positive manner to criticisms and you will feel better about yourself.

Sounds of Silence

Laying deep in your soul, tucked away from all of life's interruptions, is a golden staircase leading to your dreams. There lie your passions, your secrets, your bliss. Try and find that place every day with just a few moments of silence. Listen to what the stillness is saying to you. Get up early and watch the sunrise. Breathe in the glory of a new day.

Clear Your Mind with a Walk

A nice walk will cure most problems, refresh your soul and provide moments of serenity to clear your mind.

Give with No Expectations

Wrap up your inner self in a big red bow and give it to others.
Give of your talents, your laughter, your affection, encouragement
and love. Do not expect or require anything in return…it comes
back to you.

Limit the
Couch Time

Move, dance, play,
run, skip and soar.

What would you do if you knew you could not fail?

Imagine not having the fear to do the things you want to do in life. Today, at this very moment, you have the ability, wisdom and strength to be all you want to be and have all your dreams come true. Trust in yourself, toss the fears aside and let the hues of your bright future shine through.

- *Your greatest successes will come as a result of a previous failure.*

- *Participate in life – never withdraw.*

- *Never give up… this is not an option.*

Meditation for the Soul

Learn the art of meditation. It's a wonderful way of releasing the stresses of the day. You can start by just setting aside ten minutes at the beginning or end of each day. The ability to breathe slowly and systematically creates a relaxing physical self.

Meditation is the way to
the fountain of youth!

Greet the Day!

Enjoy the early morning hours with peace, quiet and reflection.
Take a few minutes to simply sit and breathe. The most glorious part
of the day is the sunrise when the day slowly gets brighter, when the
dark blue sky turns a lighter hue and the brilliant colors start to seep
into the sky.

Appreciate
Yourself

Your happiness and self-worth are not dependent on what others may think of you. Regardless of the challenges in your life, make the conscious decision to appreciate yourself and to completely enjoy being you, with everything this entails.

Enjoy the Journey

Goals are important but not at the expense of your happiness.
Maintain a balance between getting to where you want to go and
being happy as you get there.

Art of Nothingness

If I could teach you just one thing, it would be the art of stillness.
To calm our minds and allow the gifts of nature's bounty to caress
our soul is the ultimate in peace and tranquility. Find the beauty of
everyday things: clouds, birds, music, water, trees…

Be in the Moment

Focus on one task at a time rather than trying to accomplish everything at once.

Girls Just Want to Have Fun

- When a friend talks with you, let them be the focal point of your attention.

- When asked for advice, give it honestly, but respectfully.

- Never criticize your friend to others.

- Be patient and be there for your friend when she/he needs you.

- Choose friends regardless of age.

Mindfulness

Completely focus on the work or task before you. We find the
greatest enjoyment not when we are passively mindless but when
we are absorbed in a mindful challenge.

Be Cautious When Comparing Yourself to Others

This can sometimes make you feel good about yourself or even inspire you. However, making comparisons to others can often lead you to overlook what is truly unique about you.

Peacefulness

Do not allow life's challenges to disturb your tranquility.
Life is far too precious to be wasted on nonessential issues.

Lose Yourself in a Book

Reading can be like a mini-vacation, a mind expanding exercise that enriches our lives. Give yourself a regular time each day or once a week to read. When you find a book that you particularly enjoy, share it with a friend.

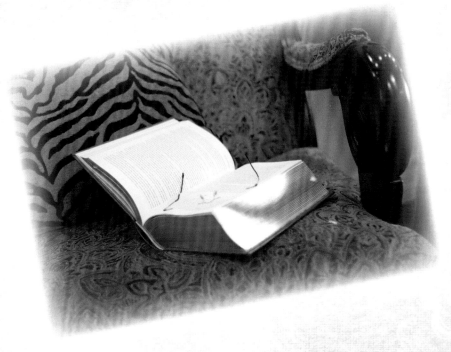

I Have Learned

I am less interested in how I look and care more about how I feel.

I do not seek perfection. I seek to be honest and true to myself… flaws and all.

To open myself to the flow of inspiration and creativity.

To laugh often, cry easily and love deeply.

To accept what I have, be happy with what I have, who I am and where I am.

Grandma is living a successful life. . .

I have loved and I have lost, I have cried many tears and I have filled my heart with laughter. I have so much more of life to live and so much more to give.

I have made mistakes and I continue to learn from them. I have made many friends and have many new ones that I have not yet met. I have danced all night in the pale moonlight and watched the sunrise after staying up all night making the clouds move and watching the stars.

I still play, laugh, sing and dance. I shall always question the unknown and rejoice in life's lessons.

May your life be full of glorious days, momentous evenings and abundant love.

Dear Granddaughter

Life Lessons from Your Grandmother

Written by Judy Smith
Photography by Lou Guarracino

Published by Holland Publishing
86 Doe Run Drive, Holland PA 18966
www.hollandpublishinggroup.com

ISBN: 978-0-615-54102-0
Library of Congress Control Number: Pending

Book and jacket design:
Peri Poloni-Gabriel, Knockout Design, www.knockoutbooks.com
Second Printing: June, 2013